BULLDOZERS
at Work

D. R. Addison

PowerKiDS
press™

New York

For my little truck experts, Deming, Riley, and Hannah

Published in 2009 by The Rosen Publishing Group, Inc.
29 East 21st Street, New York, NY 10010

First Edition

Editor: Joanne Randolph
Book Design: Greg Tucker
Photo Research: Jessica Gerweck

Photo Credits: All photos Shutterstock.com

Library of Congress Cataloging-in-Publication Data

Addison, D. R.
  Bulldozers at work / D.R. Addison. — 1st ed.
     p. cm. — (Big trucks)
  Includes index.
  ISBN 978-1-4358-2702-8 (lib. binding) — ISBN 978-1-4358-3088-2 (pbk.)
ISBN 978-1-4358-3094-3 (6-pack)
  1. Bulldozers—Juvenile literature. I. Title.
  TA735.A3185 2009
  624.1'52—dc22
                                        2008023582

Manufactured in the United States of America
CPSIA Compliance Information: Batch #113160PK: For Further Information Contact Rosen Publishing, New York, New York at 1-800-237-9932

Contents

Bulldozers are used to move dirt around. They push the dirt and make the ground even.

Bulldozers work hard all day. This bulldozer is pushing dirt onto a beach.

Bulldozers can work as part of a team. These trucks are ready to get to work!

9

Bulldozers have a big **blade** on the front to push earth around.

Some bulldozers have a smaller blade behind the big one. Do you see one here?

Some bulldozers have **crawler tracks**. The crawler tracks are like big, long wheels.

15

The crawler tracks move around small wheels. This is the same way a bike **chain** moves.

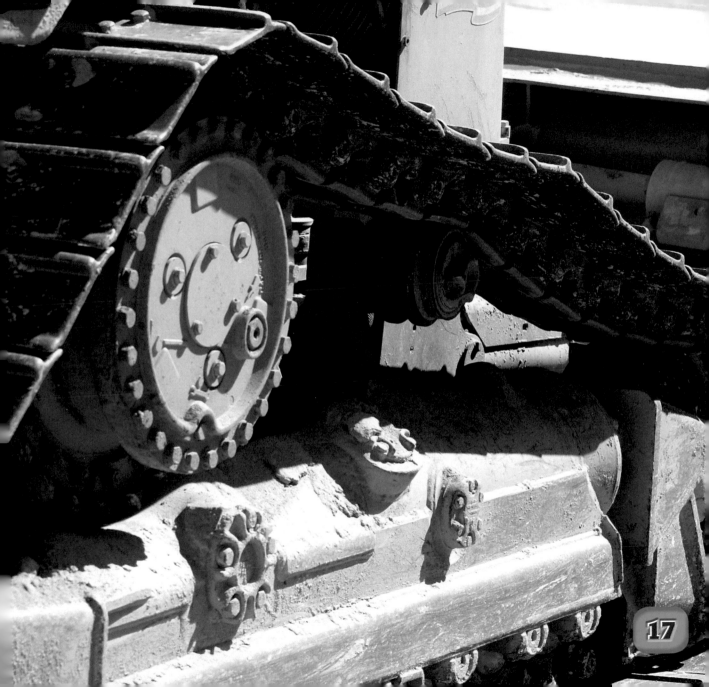

Some bulldozers have big **tires** instead of crawler tracks.

19

Above the crawler tracks sits the cab. The cab is where the driver sits.

21

Thanks for letting us watch you at work, bulldozer!